Soul to Touch

Soul to Touch

Anne Campbell

HAGIOS PRESS
Box 33024 Cathedral PO
Regina SK S4T 7X2
www.hagiospress.com

Copyright © 2009 Anne Campbell

All rights reserved. No part of this publication may be reproduced, stored in a retrieval system, or transmitted in any form or by any means without the prior written permission of the publisher or by licensed agreement with Access: The Canadian Copyright Licensing Agency. Exceptions will be made in the case of a reviewer, who may quote brief passages in a review to print in a magazine or newspaper, broadcast on radio or television, or post on the Internet.

Library and Archives Canada Cataloguing in Publication

Campbell, Anne
   Soul to touch / Anne Campbell.

Poems.
ISBN 978-1-926710-01-3

   I. Title.

PS8555.A5272S69 2009   C811'.54   C2009-904710-1

Edited by Douglas Barbour.
Designed and typeset by Donald Ward.
Cover design by Tania Wolk.
Cover art by John Noesthedan.
Cover photo by Don Hall.
Set in Adobe Caslon Pro.
Printed and bound in Canada.

The publishers gratefully acknowledge the assistance of the Saskatchewan Arts Board, The Canada Council for the Arts, and the Cultural Industries Development Fund (Saskatchewan Department of Culture, Youth & Recreation) in the production of this book.

*For my brothers, Ron, Rick, Ken, and Ray,
and for other family and friends,
especially J.M.*

I couldn't feel, so I learned to touch.
Leonard Cohen
"Hallelujah"

Contents

THE FOREST FLOOR

The Bird Beckons	11
Drought Relief	12
Light Works as Anointing Material	13
Colour Leaving Remains	14
How We May Touch	15
Gift of Breath	16
Trees Take Account of the Air	17
Rings	18
If This Reads	19
Time for Poetry	20
Late Spring Grace	21
The Grass and Me in the Morning	22
Sun Miracles	23
Two in the Sky, Me in the Grass	24
Forgetting Fear	25
Birds Die	26
Overnight, the Storm, the Sun, and the Sea	27
Sight of Trees	28
Driving Home Yesterday	29
The Gulls	30
The Nature of Loss	31
Giving Up the House	32
Today	33
As I Hurry Downtown Today	34
Everything Is Falling	35
The Small Bird Death	36
A Healthy Fear	37
Autumn	38

DRAWING

After March of the Penguins	41
The Flowers Remain	42
The Moon Draws	43
Marks Speak	44
Doing Earth Philosophy	45
St. Peter's Dinner	46
The Jesse Tree	47
The Lacquered Orchard Petrified	48
The Drawing	49
Risk	50
Red Fox	51
Swift Fox, Nearly Extinct	52
The Houses	53
Shoulder Angel Slow Down	54
The Name of the Place Was Love	55
The Artist Draws Lines, after j.	56
Falling Into the Sky	57
Bacon Lover Prayer	58

BANFF POEMS

Evergreen Mirrors my Song	61
1. Becoming: A Heart	62
2. The Discomfort with God	63
3. Chance Exchange	63
4. Falling over Myself	64
5. One	64
6. Sky Numbers	65
7. Untitled	66
8. The Deck God	66
9. Cain, Abel, and Me in Banff	67

10. The Relief	67
11. The Bassoon Class, Master Class	68
12. The Viola Player	68
13. Walking the Road after the Test	69
14. Colony Sabbath	69
Looking at the Photographs	70

FAITHFUL

Sophie in the Morning	73
The Stove and Missing You	74
Identity	75
My Friend	76
My Mother's Name is Rose	77
Victoria	78
My Heart Holds Still	79
Faithful	80
Everything is Immanent	81
Bone Naked	82
Pruning	83
At Mocha House	84
Waking up Alone	85
Time and Being	86
The Care of God	88
The Paces of Love	89
Winter (Foxes) Drawn to Light	90
Comes the Word	91
One Might Live by the Water	92
Not a Question of Love	93
A Commissioning of Words	94
Acknowledgements	95

THE FOREST FLOOR

THE BIRD BECKONS

        a small white bird circles   just above
     my left field of vision   but
           it is a tree I desire to write
          the bird circles,   and circles,
pushed away
   by my urge for something more solid   keeps circling
              nearly landing   and if

        I flick my head sideways

         she swoops down

      I tell you I *would* have her land

    but the tree   I want for her rest
         is not yet written

DROUGHT RELIEF

Grass, as we make our way home, late this day
    is ready to break from hiding   come
from under the surface, move out from straw covered   land
left bare this past winter, no snow   these patches are pale

    shadows of hope   green on the brink.

Dust devils on my left pictures in a book   divide
                           right and wrong
                   keep their distance so far

    but in the city, wind takes shape, bits of stone
    strike my face, the back of my neck, my legs

    In the morning I linger   after a night trace of rain
    carry in my mind a memory of lake, smell of the sea   and

    in the midst of this absence, forced to myself
    I see this desert as home   find in my heart   room

    my shoulders drop down

    I reach into drought   wait for rain
    to weep herself   free.

Anne Campbell

LIGHT WORKS AS ANOINTING MATERIAL

    Light works as anointing material   salves itself
                      into your body
    you can feel it in your pores
       working its way   not
                 into your heart
   might have expected that line   but

   light moves into your skull,

and your skull
       may be bruised

  light

    shoulders herself (her shoulders are large)

   shoulders herself   into your mind,

your crowded mind you can feel it there

    working its way, moving   all through your body

Soul to Touch

COLOUR LEAVING REMAINS, for A

Scotch Thistle, purple and plump   always
appealing from the side of the road
                           stems
picked in summer with gloves on my hands, wild flowers
scattered over green in a basket in my living room

flowers resting stiff as jewels
                      this winter warm me

Anne Campbell

HOW WE MAY TOUCH, after A

   Emerging high   out of cold
     prairie winter, one grand maple tree;
         relieved of snow this tree umbrellas one sprawling berry bush

Framing these precursors of spring fiercely pruned
    two smaller barren maple trees

   More than once passing in this north (land where we live)
I worry these trees; will the season last enough for them to grow? I worry
                        pruning
    too much cutting back of rot
      will make their growing slow

         But bit by bit
   in early summer, in one moment to the naked eye,
a flush of green sudden leaves in a breeze waving

          this writing now should wrap a scene of leaves
  around the tall maple tree sprawling berry bush, include

        the two maple trees blossomed late

     but these smaller trees do not reach across the sky

held apart as they are by the others
               they do not touch   but simply sway

Soul to Touch

GIFT OF BREATH

    I breathe   in

           breathe

                  in-

                      hale

this gift

    beyond

                my body

  gracious as ever

Anne Campbell

TREES TAKE ACCOUNT OF THE AIR
after St. Peter's Abbey

1.

Walking early morning across the monastery yard
    air   breathing   breeze
       ruffling dark poplar trees already

    I've walked our country road,
    eaten eggs coddled for breakfast,
found a monk who's found a tape recorder,
    my new song waiting to be sung,

    "Light works as an anointing material,
    works its way, works its way into my body . . ."

2.

    the day barely begun   but alive I hear
leaves   almost name
  the feeling   on my face they are trying
    to say: listen,   you are happy. This rustle I take to mean
        content.

3.

  Trees do not let you down,   oh their leaves bend,   and
    daily   they shake out their grief ,   but
only the rarest tornado can fell one,   pruned well they withstand
    even
      this;
  trees I think of as answers,   love
    in   solitary monastery   air

Soul to Touch

RINGS

Looking down, my right hand is without
the usual rings I wear. Both are missing

as you too giver of these rings
move into the background of my life

a place in my body where you begin to recede;
but the rings: one black pearl set high in silver

you had it made for me alone; the other a ring from your mother,
amber set in thick red gold. Rings so different from the one
                                          I wear
on my other hand common tawny coloured stone;
I found it   in valley land near here   before I knew you
had it put under gold (asked for) a setting rough

IF THIS READS

      If this reads like a self help manual,
as my aunts would say, "so be it," these, the same aunts who called
their second farm dog, blind, and no warrior, Hector;

    their first, bold, they called Gypsy   but never mind

  I'm leaving it all to the gods   making no decision
  waiting for distraction   to lose you
to the world ... remember that last time
                your leaving
     slowly ached out of me   my hurt skin all my body cells
             ... *assimilate*
  not a word that passes the test of poetry
        but *assimilate* is a word   and I could feel it then
taking
     grief from me, high into the air I could feel it all around me
         in bits of time in the air   dissolving

Soul to Touch

TIME FOR POETRY

The time for poetry has ended now
I just want you in my bed, pure and simple, not
   your sex only you for me to curl round
      for the time being

Anne Campbell

LATE SPRING GRACE

Not one, not two, but three
rabbits, still white this cool spring evening leap and
leap   in front of my car I imagine they continue

all through town

Wanting to leave a man alone I have
parked my car not by our city's man-made lake
but on the banks of this old country creek   which feeds it.

These rabbits then must not they have meaning
give voice to choice parked in a car by a creek?   But

I am distracted
       evening sky so blue light dropping   gulls
                         swooping in every direction

   only when I look back and

  down to the grass do I shield my eyes
  sun striking my car at a slant   *blinding.*

THE GRASS AND ME IN THE MORNING
after St. Michael's

Walking again I always start the words
walking
grass tall by the side of the road   tall
by the side of the road that makes its way up the hill   where
Franciscans live
and writers retreat   inside bodies   and   roads
lead everywhere

but back
to the tall green grass   beside me as I walk:

do the blades, each, as I do,
think *to themselves s*eeing me beside their prairie nest, on a hill,
does grass think: *does it not*

make sense to think

we, the grass (speaking for itself) and (me) the woman walking
are in love
breathing in and out of one another   this morning
a marriage   with the prairie   grass at ease

Anne Campbell

SUN MIRACLES

Waking and turning out of my bed,
the T-shirt I draped over my curtain yesterday

this morning pure white
the stain that remained
so long *after scrubbing* gone

a small miracle
my mind makes so but no
the T-shirt all afternoon

bleached in the sun;
it was only I saw this
miracle   over night

TWO IN THE SKY, ME IN THE GRASS, St. Michael's

Today it isn't walking I do my companion her name   grief,
wishes only to lie down, not walk the wild hills my way;
I look for a sign a way to arrest her wound   but she closes my eyes, says,
I need all your attention, lie down on this grass, imagine you're home
take care of me still. And I do, lie on the grass on the side of a hill,
forget about time   I may even sleep.

A narrative line wants to come into this poem   can you imagine space
in the middle of time

when I open my eyes up to the sky I think
it must be a hawk flying so high swooping in circles
behind clouds and I follow, and follow   then there are two
hawks in the air swooping and arcing   and lifting
a skim from my heart leaving a wound open to air and
tomorrow   two of a kind watch   as I pass
deer on the path   we cross.

Anne Campbell

FORGETTING FEAR, St. Peter's

        Walking
    through (man-planted) pine
so tall, in straight lines, underbrush clear
        here   at the Abbey
          I forget fear   and coming out of woods
            upon a meadow greet purple
      daisy-like flowers, wild (Fringed American-Aster)
   floating above tiny   golden bulbs
              (Pineappleweed)   and
what does it all mean   heart lifted so everything changing as it does

Soul to Touch

BIRDS DIE, Writing Colony

Here, away from home, fourth day
    a family beginning to jell
over lunch we tell stories: our animals at home
      gifts we have been given and Corky the deep yellow
      Canary you brought home that first Christmas serves both.

    You saw the birds in my house painted on walls
resting on tables, images aplenty, surmised I was missing
           only the real.

    For seven years we co-existed, Corky and me,
        afraid to touch (his) Sunday bath
    the closest we came to losing fear he seldom sang
                    but
in the weeks before he died, he did sing
and sing   loud and clear
        all day long   he sang
      and our hearts rose together;
   until one morning   Corky was gone and

   this all happened years ago   but as I tell the story now
     you too long gone finally
        I am weeping

Anne Campbell

OVERNIGHT, THE STORM, THE SUN AND THE SEA

    On the sea storms reel toss and
  turn water high
        but sea rolls with the punches
    and storm carries on loves
   the play of light on water.   Thunder rolls too

but sun waits
       tired
           sometimes thinks
           just to fall down   lie.
              But she likes the sea
loves a good storm
  so she waits
       waits for a break in the sky

SIGHT OF TREES, after TL

        Silent bark of tree
    wishes to be touched:

      in a green forest land
        moss and wild blue petals   carpet
the earth   a royal flush of leaves and trees
       come into being

DRIVING HOME YESTERDAY

        Stunned by the prairie
                yesterday

green and shining grasses   bending

arched beneath sky, blue scented so fresh, and
      this barely begins
   to draw the surround that loosed my heart, stilled

my mind driving home   another
      funeral; my old aunts dying
   one by one   I couldn't write this

but today, a seminar, I picked up this pen — for distraction — and

    prairie fell into place   my mother   alive
 in my memory of summer
      wheat fading to gold   bruised ripe
    the scent of fall   autumn smoke
     the wonder of it
     an actual place,
a real location my body calls home.

Soul to Touch

THE GULLS

     Walking round the lake,
  if it happens to be dusk, or just before,
gulls go crazy shrilling to each other and the sky
   shrieking in fear of light ending forever
      calling: stay stay   oh   light
                    stay

next day
    again at dusk, there they are, calling light remain   or

    is it night they call: dark draw us in
    protect us from prey 'til morning
    let us be safe another day

Anne Campbell

THE NATURE OF LOSS

      Lying in bed this morning
          empty of hope
imagination   gone silent
   missing a picture: the way horses lean into one another

necks rubbing   as the wind
          carries on around them,
                   or the way
a tiny bee loses himself deep in the heart of a golden flower

GIVING UP THE HOUSE

What it comes down to isn't the up-keep
    though that's a point,
        no
            it's the illusion
this house contains: beyond reason it holds
more years to come or at least it did
until last night when the furies arrived, sat before me
looked me straight in the eye, wasted my soul,
roused my own rage at age
Gods take away everything: smooth face of skin, energy of bone,
    delight of eye, oh yes houses they leave

Anne Campbell

TODAY, for Nonie

Driving home
        through perfection this day   we have chosen,
                my brother and me,
           a memorial, stone and text,
        to mark our parents' passing;
     we speak for the others not present

On this day then driving through wonder my *life*
        "… you can't write a poem about life." But
          I do   want to be God, draw soft blue sky above me
            draw it down and up again   and over
        until blue covers me and my car and the land all around
     I want to shade in golden earth pencil in precisely
   Highway #11, between Regina and Saskatoon   endless
 prairie, the middle of this continent
                    floating. But
prairie is not endless   it will stop   to the west
                 run into mountains begin to roll   become
rock,
    and to the east
               prairie flows into river and lake   north
   is boreal   forest   before tundra and
      south
             prairie
simply spills over a border   becomes separate   another country and
   finally
       rolls into the sea   drawing salt
           brushes and pens   brushes and pens

Soul to Touch

AS I HURRY DOWNTOWN TODAY

        Through the park
     walking fast   downtown
         first spring day   I pass a woman
           walking carefully clearly
            her degenerative body
dis-ease
         slows her but see   she is
                at ease
      and I imagine her:
carrying her books back to a library, as she does,
breathing this warm morning air, feeling
            compassion for me
       rushing past   as I do.

Anne Campbell

EVERYTHING IS FALLING

    and in the booth

in the Thai café I am eating delicious curry spiced coconut milk

    rice soup

In the next booth, *proselytizing*, a man is (actually) giving chapter and verse

    the reason why his companion

    should join   the man's faith ... rituals

I refrain from dropping my head to the table   consider

    standing up

        walking

    past the table, catching the eye of the man listening

shaking my head

    no

        don't ask for proof

further down the aisle

in another booth, two more men, oblivious: "What do you expect?"

    one is saying. "It's life," the other advises.

THE SMALL BIRD DEATH

        Oh God,
   I'm tired   sore throat   long cold coughing   and
this afternoon coming back to work, late, another meeting I try to rush
round three women   gasping, gathered, looking down   and on the
sidewalk
               iridescent, head severed from body
     small   marine-coloured bird   spilled
  on snow   Oh, God   I can't stop this can't will myself
        to imagine   this   separation
      body from soul   partner dove moaning
          from a ledge high above

     in my bones, a scream   earlier   today
             already my throat forming
        this
      dying
        my mother's sister, this Sunday
crying, Why is this taking so long? and this shriek roaming in me
     I can't stop this   dying
  I know
      Freud said: it's really fear of life, this fear of dying but
          did he remember this when he died,
  and the monks who say, it's all part of life,   a nice lesson
       I knew a monk once
     fluid rising in his lungs fought
until he drowned amazing the others who thought surely this man
was one
           ready to go
        the mind then the mind
     comes to terms with dying, sometimes   but the body
  the beautiful body   wants to live wants so badly just to live
                              forever
       breathing the God-damned wonderful air

A HEALTHY FEAR

God is not the Hound of Heaven but a great
grandmother standing still while a plump
feathered chicken flies in circles fearing this mother touch;
it could be too she'll nestle *you* in the crook of her arm
drawing you near for further action.

AUTUMN

        leaves are turning

        a fall shade of red:

it used to be thought   this deep red signaled death

                a tree passing

but now scientists say this red released drives insects away

        high energy, "as much

as you'd expect of a sapling still young," they say

            which

    makes no sense to me — suggesting, as it does, insects welcome

            by tender green but

      the point, the point of this poem is

      energy   a tree ready for winter

        the last of her strength

drawn

    to a sign beyond even the power of her youth

DRAWING

AFTER MARCH OF THE PENGUINS

    Seeing *March of the Penguins*
   their walk 70 miles inland   from sea
  little tuxedo-dressed men and women   drawn
by instinct five years afterwards to the place of their birth.

I think of the stories we used to tell: how we met, twice; the first time
      each alive to the other, in a café, not imagining
            we'd meet again

        Then four or five years later
a dance performance, each of us aware at first sight, you
        liked the way I took the lead
        seating my little group   later
  a reception, I sought you out, the rest, as they say, history,
             which it seems
          we are becoming

the thing though, this instinct thing, walking back to the place of birth

to breed
            seeing someone meant to be that second birth,
                that instinct.

THE FLOWERS REMAIN, after Joyce Wieland

    The vase of water
  holds raspberry colored Freesia:
flowers in my bay window behind my kitchen sink

    I change water daily   discard petals
                  falling away

and when I turn back to the flowers they stand at ease
resting now, the few, in much remaining green

Anne Campbell

THE MOON DRAWS, after Rae Johnson

      The moon draws   oh yes
            she can draw all right
    I've seen her at night slipping to earth
  gathering roots and stone   to make her paints

she piles on colour thick green and blue she paints thin
            trunks of trees   men too
she draws forward to her own (white) reflection in water   and
                                    black
earth shadows she slicks back from trees while her men hold on for
                                                  dear life
urged to the water   drawn there by the moon
    but see though she has created this earth rolling
      she has those shadows hold everything still.

Soul to Touch

MARKS SPEAK, after Ron Bloore

        White on white marks:
           and
"The holy spirit is everywhere," Sister Everesta, my teacher
    far back in school:
        "There isn't a place you can hide
          from the love of God."

        White on white
    spirit seeps in everywhere all around and
from the centre of this painting (in space left blank
                        by the artist)

    the shape of a key, and light   trembles

Anne Campbell

DOING EARTH PHILOSOPHY

    He says he's doing philosophy, but it looks to me   like stairs:
        he's building stairs   that lead to other

                              stairs

          going up, up and away
                            from earth

and the philosophy I want is one that
    falls
        down

into fissures   where chance is the answer
                      and the earth is warm

ST. PETER'S DINNER

At the dinner party sitting across from me
a young man maps the world on cloth, tells me
he thinks in symbol, though travelling in France earlier in the year
to his boyhood home he'd searched and found not symbol
but colour and shape the way a child would feel his way
in the morning on the streets of his own small town, but for now
he still teaches his old way still finds only words
hold meaning; but surely, *I lean* it's our bodies that teach
the texture of our souls that touch our red hearts beating.

THE JESSE TREE, after the Sacrament of Reconciliation

    The Jesse tree in church tonight is loaded with *man-made fruit*
            hundreds of tiny gilt boxes tied
        to limbs of a winter grey tree hope
    brought indoors *summer reconciling*

We are told as we enter into this circle of sacrament to come forward
        and absolved from sin   to choose a box,
    open it to the word   find inside
        our very own gift   and
my box is pale ochre and blue, the cover a picture of Mary,
        the mother of God, and inside
        the word printed simple and clear
            Love
    I cannot say the perfection I feel.

All of this late the same day I have taken a pen, written freely
    my heartfelt wrongs, seeing as I did
        the only sin —
though harm may be done to others — is against *the coming to life of* oneself.

    These were the words to say.

The service continues to a close and moving to gather my things
    I see my box has been bent. More
    curious than surprised I re-form the handmade box
    love the idea of (it) being somewhat bent and

    I am telling you this story now: the perfection of a word
printed in the bottom of a box, *Love*, somewhat bent but holding   still

Soul to Touch

THE LACQUERED ORCHID PETRIFIED, after J.

1.

    Lay it down
  in a shallow bowl let it lie there flat.
Seeing me quizzical, he continues,
    otherwise you'll have to find something
sharp, project it from a wall, place the orchid
        (stem) over it, to hold.

2.

  Days later looking at this same orchid lacquered
twenty five times over sitting low in a Japanese bowl,
    male member formed carefully at its heart,
            erect

   or seen from another perspective a tiny man in cap
            and gown and
  across from him seeming
to be seen by this man a vulva quite clearly waving. Though

3.

      perhaps these waving shapes are leaves
         from a book
   this man *could be a woman* read from
as one or the other two now (be) hold pages opening before them.

Anne Campbell

THE DRAWING

The drawing where I live is pale,
a kind of ripe autumn gold, a shade of wheat
bronze in colour.

You can see me there
if you look carefully, see

just at the edge a small shape,
once shaded dark outlined now
but still needing to be filled in.

RISK

This is really the nub, that moment
giving up all: going out into the cold
northern forest I call home Beginning

    I fasten on a small red fox, a closed mother door,
    house as my lover, which one leads me which way home.

RED FOX

I've read through the whole book, it wasn't difficult
    really: catlike canine, the idea of a red that glows,

burnished brick,

    sometimes crossed with black, sandy when young,
        having charcoal natal fur,
      a natural predator over ages lasting

    the first one (*Red*)

moved me to further search,
and I found the other, *Swift*, had grown separate over the years
its family becoming   slightly different.

SWIFT FOX, NEARLY EXTINCT, for DG Jones

    There are other animals
more appealing, more easily sweet, you might say,
        valiant but oh
      Swift Fox you capture me

      not so much I agree with you
    in fact your fox eyes I do not prefer

It's the idea: you even have paws, cross-over
    Canine body close to cat

In certain light, ears spread beyond your tiny body, bat, in silhouette
    illusive Basenji Egyptian dog.

Most people, my lover says, use nature as metaphor for mood
    but you are metaphor for wild and.

  what does any of this mean; an idea of God, mystery
in which we live everything mixed nothing so clearly separate
    as we might think.

Anne Campbell

THE HOUSES

While my own body, my work
children wait, my homes take shape.

I create order, repair houses, want them to be all around
in their deepest rooms *complete* a place for soul to grow

SHOULDER ANGEL SLOW DOWN

. . . someone is saying an angel sits on her left shoulder
    and it all comes clear to me the pain just below and

    inside my left shoulder blade the way I persist,
        against all advice, in raising
that shoulder: to give (my) angel a clear view as we walk the halls, maybe
hoping she'll fall over, and off?

    Either way she's demanding

did I mention she's gaining weight must be twice as heavy now
    as when she settled in. And I think she's forgotten
    she has a job, for goodness sake the least she can do
        is give minimal affection, well to be fair,
    she does, or at least did once save me
pulled me back from a thousand pounds of horse galloping past
    as I entered
        a riding ring
    and more than once
        caught me in a car before I hit another.

    It's time though, for a talk a reunion of sorts,
she needs a change as much as me, a walk will do us both good she
                                really is
    getting heavy and since it seems she's here to stay
    to begin dropping some weight   might lighten our load.

Anne Campbell

THE NAME OF THE PLACE WAS LOVE

Remember you've been to that country the one you thought
    you'd travelled before   this time entered by accident
        only later   recognized love

Now years since you left (you left)   leafing   through a catalogue
a T-shirt, *The Art of Canoeing*, think honeymoon, parents in a canoe,
photograph,
    the perfect gift for him who canoed,
  to mark that time   together but (time doesn't end)

The catalogue rests by the phone a week   and
   during the days you remember the peace of it all wonder
how you came so close: walking into the place
   too wounded to fabricate, not able to lie, this
    the cause of the same in him?

The two of us in that place not yearning
not even "hot" for one another, never were   both of us
surprised by the science of it all   a field of peace created
between us in the space we found beyond our separate selves.

This T-shirt then, the one with the canoe, I choose as a gift
for him and for my mother and my father who entered that place
and me who re-members   that mystery

Soul to Touch

THE ARTIST DRAWS LINES, after J.

   How
to write the lines the breath of God
       100, one thousand
    the aahhh
        of release   lines
            drawn
              down
                that dull glow   repeated and repeated, and
              all the other lines
                surely

Anne Campbell

FALLING INTO THE SKY, after Emily Dickinson

Saying yes   to a poem
about Emily,   writing her back or   simply
responding   the invitation said   simply respond   and   Emily is
                       slipping   out of her house   to her porch
         at dusk   coupling   with the tender night air   in love
she glows

      can't keep it straight   doesn't even try   she mixes her words
        with birds   and God   the air we all breathe   and

my grandson, Thomas, says: the world is turning
      everything moving   so fast
          a person could fall into the sky   Emily   too

   is falling
in love   with the sting of a star screaming past   afraid
she writes   every particle of the world touching her skin   and the sky

      this cold winter: Emily's words   soft as stones   (set down
         on a summer   cloth)   slip into my heart
                       undivided
      she writes   the birds of the sky   the stars
        she writes   the very air   together.

Soul to Touch

BACON LOVER PRAYER, after Catherine Bush

You are gone   oh yes
        we may unite again but there is emptiness
            coming into this house

            in the evening:
        your absence is strong   but

this morning, Sunday, when we might have been making love
  I am eating reheated bacon on thin crisp toast   reading
        a review of a book that contains
    my migraine malady that strange land of colour

      but it's the bacon I feel   how truly good
    this sandwich   taste rising as it does in this moment
moving through me and above everything this pleasure
        deserving its own small praise

BANFF POEMS

EVERGREEN MIRRORS MY SONG

    Turning the corner
        en route over mountain roads
           music in my car
                Buffy Marie singing from her throat
                and before me
                    mirroring her vibration,
                        herringbone row upon row
                                              evergreen
trees repeat and
  beside me
     the head of a single yellow rose
        I carry this totem from one
            not easily given to the practice of love

                but today slipping through sun
                    my heart is in his hands driving

1. BECOMING: a heart

Walking in the early steep
part of the path on Sleeping Buffalo
some still call it Tunnel Mountain
it comes to me to write
when I get back to my room: no matter
which way you cut it I am
a woman, without doubt
I have breasts and though small
they did give forth at least once

I plan
still breathing (too) hard to write
more of me, a man in me
as I walk, the one
whose picture I scribble over
each time he begins to hint a shape

then here at a corner
near the top, stopped in a bit of shade
for breath on the tree I lean against
directly at eye level
not carved but worn away in a shade of rust, a heart
its colour deeper than its pale rose shape surround.

What to make of it: male and female and a heart, *rose*, and the note
back in my studio quoting a writer asking me to read
the signs, and the other one: *writing, is writing, is writing,*
all this on my path, sun unusually hot
without clouds this year for tempering
cedar berries lush for the picking when suddenly
ill with it all
I turn slowly   back and down
hoping for time   to return.

2. THE DISCOMFORT WITH GOD

Veering near the idea of God, even the word: I am not

in comfort   wish to avoid the slight ache
            these images create
        in my body   I sense
    a risk of treading too close to the bone. This feeling
        tied too with more confusion over male
        and female wanting to break that barrier

3. CHANCE EXCHANGE

This morning a gift of cloud
before I rise to the day unprepared
for beginning I seek coffee
and by chance two travelers
unlikely messengers via New York

talk of art and nature
of being, cities, keeping pace and
before I do they bring in God and

when they leave these unlikely
angels have left me
an image, concrete, city as male;
grass fallen in nature, female
folding softly over herself

Soul to Touch

4. FALLING OVER MYSELF

    Grass in nature, lasting long
    but growing only so high
               carried by the weight of itself
                      falling
                         down

        down
              and gently over
                              blades

  resting on one another   a family at ease.

5. ONE

Male and female, each with a piece of the action, one
concrete, white or grey depending
on the mix of minerals those particles they add to give colour to
stone. Too much in the mix bruises elbows and cheeks
sends a body to pasture for relief, a woman's heart offering rest

in this season grass bending in on itself untouched but
by elk who gather each morning
at my studio in the woods where for weeks I've been circling, afraid
of secrets lying shallow my mother, *Rose,* brought forth,

my mother in the middle of a metaphor of nature and
the earth; a gesture of one's own kind   contained

between beginning and before   tall grass

leans over herself resting her surplus
but she is not boundless; concrete is

moving out from the centre of cities
covering land   and my heart stops   worrying the sound
passing   and passing   and another one passes

the trees, some are dead but still stand rooted for years
shadows on grass   untouched but by elk
who pass on their way deep into woods.

6. SKY NUMBERS

Walking into the woods to my waiting studio, silence fills my pores,
working here everything is possible; the number of my studio is one.

My room number, on the other hand, is nine,
a number either a) waiting forever to act: a bear
sleeping the long winter through or b) if luck is willing, wakened
moving strong, always at an angle, present on the page.

One though is an eagle
                soaring
                            high in the air

 coming back only for young
 waiting to feed   fledglings in a nest

Soul to Touch

7. UNTITLED

God is
(man and woman grass and
concrete)
    constraint
  constructed
        minerals
lifted from mountains
deposited in factories for fuelling

cities for living (loving) and escape

to green where elbows and shoulders
drop down where faces soften leaving the good
male god concrete behind.

8. THE DECK GOD

I sit on my deck   today
circling in on God
from behind my studio watch grass reach up; shoots
rest each on one another   leaning forward they bend
in places where elk nest lay their great bodies down

      today
beginning is
full of cloud   but warmed beyond hope touched
by this gift   my soul is making (concrete) words whole

Anne Campbell

9. CAIN, ABEL, AND ME IN BANFF

The story of these two sons
confuses me   I read the story again:

Cain and Abel, and my own mixed blessings
    entering that unknown   space

inside the mix of me   a man
and a woman   I'm not of course
except that we all are whole
notes of God (Mozart heard this
writing music even for the tiny timpani)

it was Cain I found slew Abel *the* brother
who made a better offering of sheep
sent away for this, though strangely,
blessed with a sign to keep him safe.

10. THE RELIEF

I feel now an idea of God man and woman each one
part of the whole urge to reason set aside
flowers in a field blowing free
   hawk   roaming
  wing foreshadowing

Soul to Touch

11. THE BASSOON CLASS, master class

> Banff mountain morning room sunny after rain students
> near the end of their time three weeks
> with a teacher who schools them well: has them
> spinning deep into notation
> creating just the right sound
> one particular to each because
>
> music, he says, is waiting
> in each bassoon for a player's intention
>
> the audience too: we are waiting
> ready for the music in our bones

12. THE VIOLA PLAYER

Later I would see she was unusually tall, her nature
a weather warning bleak

For a change I faced this; stared her ill manners down
spoke about my affection for the viola,
an instrument she played. Why, she asked, and when I said I resonated
to the sound, she asked again, why. And I turned
the question, asked the same of her. It sounds awful, she said, played badly
but played well it's necessary to the orchestra. No one
picks it out as something special but if it's missing you know it's gone.

It links all the other instruments, like its partner the bassoon
it's not spectacular but it is necessary for connection.

13. WALKING THE ROAD AFTER THE TEST

Remember the last time
I checked: found
that left unused side of my body
strong, the right side, weak   and today
years later
checking again a fitness consultant
shows me my upper body,
I'd planned to correct,
exceptionally fit. Now the weakness
appears not so much in my heart
but in my lower body, back movement, frail.

14. COLONY SABBATH

1.

Why do I love the weekends, even here
where I can write
all day long, every day, any moment
that moves me.

2.

But when Saturday arrives
I settle
in a way nothing disturbs.

3

Where in my body is this history
this voice   calling for rest

LOOKING AT THE PHOTOGRAPHS
                    for Joseph, Jacqueline and Jill

    The snapshots of these three kids   move me
                to a kind of joy
           I cannot speak

these bodies
        ache in me: my jaw, shoulders, throat all
              feel   these angels
      turning their heads up to me from sand,
camping holidays,
    birthday dinners;
      I cannot find words to say the love reaching over years
            to touch me   now.

FAITHFUL

SOPHIE IN THE MORNING

She knows what she needs:
in the morning   she wants to be held
more specifically wants to lay herself down on your chest and purr
raise her head from time to time
look you directly in the eye, she knows
when to leave
in the evening
she calls quite clearly
"hold me"   and again

when she's had enough she leaves
there is an urge to draw this metaphor more clear
as though you don't know

THE STOVE and missing you

New kitchen counters bring my kitchen, into this century
                or at least,
        move it and me to . . . well, change is hard.
Now
        a new stove, "top of the line," surface glass
                cooks and warms things with control.
                    What more
                could a woman ask?   But
        next day walking into my house the stove accosts me
                longing rises: *I want my old stove back,*
want to call the *Refit* Store want to pick up the phone and   only
    the family the stove has descended to keeps me from the call.

              I do not want a new stove in my house
                                      but it is here   and

I search for a pot, a red one, place it on the surface   go out the door fast
search a store   find towels   red ones   hang one on the oven door think
                    time will tell   time will tell
                and in case you think this loss
            not real   that it lacks logic   all of this story is true.

Anne Campbell

IDENTITY

    I think I might be
        turning
  normal
that strangeness I ordinarily feel is missing

      I appear to be
  almost well though a peculiar kind of confusion is in me
  out here all alone inner watcher at rest.

Who's in charge, I wonder, when I ponder
                getting to know
       who it is I think
      I am
  wanting to know what "makes me tick"
a question
       of wisdom, or   Adam and Eve wanting to *know*
         the face of god

Soul to Touch

MY FRIEND

    Remember that feeling   being in a place
where everything is free comes when you *really*
                                                      love
  give up desire   (for) having it all and

                all around you the earth
          gives back   everything, then

         you think
maybe it's not the man you love but the earth
                      giving up

  Oh the man a gift to be grateful for   surely

Anne Campbell

MY MOTHER'S NAME IS ROSE

In this poem,
I water roses   in a garden by the sea   roses
dusted to protect them
              from insects eating

Back home on the prairie I do nothing
absolutely nothing for my roses   oh
cut them back a bit in the fall and they grow
my roses grow   now I remember my mother
bring her into this poem

VICTORIA, birthday

    I used to write a poem on my birthday an annual
    welcome to myself so to speak and today

    here by the sea near a duck pond and a bridge
                   a long way from my north and
        prairie home
  I do write

More peaceful
        than ever   and
            I have known peace:

    once long ago when night terror
      seized me in sleep too deep to survive

        I felt myself slipping away   and
        as I was falling felt
  someone entering, filling my room, me, filling everything
  with such peace *its texture was velvet* but

    what does any of this mean this
  grace that story here by the sea   those I love at home

Anne Campbell

MY HEART HOLDS STILL

    The right thing to do if you love   and I do
    is let go the right thing to do if you love

        send him on his way, wish him well, set him free

I have done all of this, even said the words   out loud.
  It's my heart won't let go beyond any sense
      my heart holds him   still.

FAITHFUL

From the beginning we fought
like cats and dogs, or a dog and a cat, or
any such combination we fought tooth and nail

he had diversions, young women
make men feel good

and me: remember the stories, women whose husbands
went to sea   never to return some of them believed

men would come back and that hope
kept them alive;   even today this happens

  and   just now

looking up to cross the street   wondering
the best way to turn (thinking, set the man free
let him be)   the Film Director in me
has me walk straight ahead and   truly
when I look up the Street sign says   *Faithful*

EVERYTHING IS IMMANENT, after A.

1.

  At the Butchart Gardens this spring
      millions of buds are pulsing
         crowded inside
petals of colour   near bursting and
on this well tended path   my body feels
      such longing,
you with me here   and this garden would be
        animated

2.

Today, another garden, the Abkhazi
  more gentle than yesterday red
lichen furled tight against rock succulent   lips
        pursed to the sky
  your absence shadowing me

        escaping

3.

  like my mother finding comfort in a Cathedral
    I find my way to a picture gallery:
        and these paintings
      still my soul
      bring me back   and all things missing

4.

        pale
      in the face of these man made creations
         and lichen
    the way cells find a pattern   hold memory
   tight to rock   plump themselves up   to light

BONE NAKED

        Here's an idea: walking
            always walking
                    now
        away from home
        you might say   lost or

more simply
    alone: anchors
        in dry dock under
        lock and key I am

only lonely for familiar   *identity*
my history   made naked

Anne Campbell

PRUNING

    African Violets pruned
    (last resort) but somewhat ordinary:

    a way to avoid
    words
    unlocking — the kids say: *don't*
                               go there but

    for the grace of God I would have gone saved
                                         for now

    by coffee walks   housework   and
                        God slips into my mind
    how boring it must be   forever pruning

AT MOCHA HOUSE at fisherman's wharf

In my favorite place   by the window
on a high stool I can see ships at bay
looking up from my coffee, *The Globe and Mail,*
I see across the water women walking dogs

here workers smoke cigarettes in front of the café
regulars inside for company or
a respite from company then

in a flurry of colour, swishing past   a group of walkers
    sorting chairs   in front of my window

they are shining their financial well being
polished   jackets   muted   plaid
sandy suede the men with hats have paid
a pretty penny   their grey hair
cut to frame them best and their faces
all of their faces unusually
uniform the men as soft as the gentle angles
of their bustling women and seeing them thus
how easy to imagine *nothing*: no loss has touched them,
no strength was needed, no foot stepped out from pain,
judges, finance men, professors, an odd engineer
it would be easy their difference from me clear but
it's plain to see we are all here   together
we breathe the same air.

Anne Campbell

WAKING UP ALONE

    At first *dawning; no, the dawn comes later*
           at first   waking
              everything as usual as though beside me
  lies a man
I would spend the day with   spend the day
 its coins: another body   walking with me in the sun
    by the sea and all the other *trivialities* he called
my coffee, walk by the water, music: Martha Wainwright, and her brother,
Rufus
   singing,
        but as I stretch   truly waken
        today my streets waken too and
        in bits of my body
        tiniest cells are becoming

TIME AND BEING

        Here alone:
           there being nothing else to be   I am
       here alone   reading   and reading   *negation*

         Heidigger, being German, has   on *his* own
hit upon
       what Buddhists — not to mention farmers in their fields —
      call *detachment,* that fortunate space *one may be given,* not
knowing
        answers,   or even questions,

that moment   (alone)

   when warm air strikes your face, that's *the warm air*
      created by the earth   going round and round
           nowhere but

  nonetheless turning   in earnest   turning and asking
           has someone removed the rail
          I was meant to ride upon?

      the earth turning and turning, until
                one thing after another,
        all things wear out,
   once in awhile *seeing an opportunity* the earth
        shifts

Anne Campbell

      just for a moment
    and stepping back
every
 thing
    falls
      cells lie quiet

  all we know is at rest
     and in this

   empty

(Heidegger calls negation) all springs forth

THE CARE OF GOD

    Do I misread the prayer, "turn myself
      over
    to the care of God."   Turn myself over?   I've

turned myself over all right   twisted   and turned myself

over and out of shape   or into shape . . . well, enough of that
                                            (well enough?)

bored with the bother of us   but now the instruction:

turn myself over to his care; take care of God, *look after him?*

    That's a big order, or does my (mis)
                        reading mean,

as he leaves I am to watch him go   keep that idea more or less alive.

Anne Campbell

THE PACES OF LOVE, after r.

You don't know at first when you meet them,
angels on the job; one landed here I'm pretty sure he was old Archangel Gabriel:

> he didn't mention his name *uses another one for earth*
> *not to draw attention* though he's very tall.

You can tell

> they've been here by the *upsidedownway* you feel.   He

> *shook the best of me together*
> took me through the twists and turns
> pace of love but you can't marry an angel
> (Arch or otherwise) *wings get in the way* and besides
> all things end   though strangely   I found in him myself
> strangely able   to *let go*   love from afar

> come to think of it   *being an angel*
> *he's not likely to be lost*

Soul to Touch

WINTER
(FOXES) DRAWN TO LIGHT, for r.

Winter begins in my body &
        in this shift of seasons
           my body   wants
    to lean
        into you or an idea I have of you
           in a far north land
      where white
            covers   everything and
snow
  falls
      on stone and trees   and small forest foxes
are drawn
      over thin crusts of ice
          to light shining from a place
you are
      making a home and it's this idea   I am leaning into
            winter dwelling

Anne Campbell

COMES THE WORD

      This body
      almost all of it   water
      in this body   something
            is born
    an idea takes shape   no idea
          how
      the impulse
urge to speak *best way to track* a shadow swims in your body
        through flesh and bone
        mostly water
to cords strung so perfect   in your throat with breath
        and tongue *sound*:   through your body
                your mind   god, shifting position

Soul to Touch

ONE MIGHT LIVE BY THE WATER

There comes a time
                someone has set these words
    music
      drifts into me   but there does come a time
                to think of moving on
it could be a gift   the chance of a lifetime   but old habits die hard
          not easy to leave a house you love.
You think maybe another city a smaller place,
                    an apartment   but nothing
                            suffices
Then one day driving a familiar road
you mark in your mind your body stirring
              driving into the sun and past a place
           you've seen many times *before*
        grasses and paths   a bit of the wild
            green, and water all in
   your own home town:
          whether or not you could find a place here
                  is a matter of conjecture
but at least for now you know
     there is some kind of wild   close at hand you *could* call home

Anne Campbell

NOT A QUESTION OF LOVE, after A.

    We loved our dad   us kids
        nothing
could stop us   but when he wanted a companion
for his wild prairie rides
       we declined.

      Not that you are my dad or even
         for that matter a drinker:
you have other issues *don't we all* so   though I can't stop
       loving you

    neither can I
  join you for one of those rides   a life time long

Soul to Touch

A COMMISSIONING OF WORDS,

>   after the Art Gallery of Regina

    Make
small marks on paper put down code unlock colour   with words

                waiting
        to shape   the space we need to see:

my mother under duress
    my mother under the word duress   praying the rosary each evening
      with her sister she fingers her beads roped together they touch
           the sides of her hands, keeping calm.   And

        each person in the world,   *I see*
     laying hands each upon a particular bead   and
       into each bead unraveling the weight of their fear   grey
        held tight against a pale shade of hope and
  lying in bed undone these nights
I think of my mother and her sister   lying silent
       reach for a pen   make marks on this page   shape words
         one after another
               but tonight not words   only

       intention   gesture of arm   staying the course
you can see there for yourself on the wall beyond black is light.

Anne Campbell

ACKNOWLEDGEMENTS

The author thanks the Saskatchewan Arts Board for their funding of the Saskatchewan Writers Guild Writers/Artists Colonies and, as well, the Leighton Colony at Banff, for providing the opportunity to work without distraction. Thanks to DG (Doug) Jones, Kevin Burns, and Leona King for early readings and detailed responses. Thanks to Douglas Barbour for his close and sensitive editing, and to Hagios Press for their commitment to poetry. Thanks also to artists Don Hall and John Noesthedan, and to my dear friends and family, both siblings and children, for their ongoing support.

The poem, "Trees Take Account of the Air," was published in the anthology, *Listening with the Ear of the Heart* (St. Peter's Press, 2003). "Falling into the Sky" was performed at Emily Dickinson evenings in Regina: at Chapters in 2002 and at the Mackenzie Art Gallery in 2009. "A Commissioning of Words" was performed a part of an exhibition at the Art Gallery of Regina in 2001.

Anne Campbell's poetry, fiction, and non-fiction have appeared in magazines, journals, and anthologies nationally and internationally. She is the author of four previous collections of poetry: *No Memory of a Move* (1983), *Death is an Anxious Mother* (1986), *Red Earth, Yellow Stone* (1989), and *Angel Wings All Over* (1994). More recently, she co-edited, with Jeannie Mah and Lorne Beug, the award-winning *Regina's Secret Spaces: Love and Lore of Local Geography* (2006). She has worked at the Mackenzie Art Gallery and the Glenbow Museum, and for over 20 years was an administrator with the Regina Public Library. She is presently a Research Fellow at the Canadian Plains Research Centre, University of Regina. *Soul to Touch* is her fifth collection of poetry.